Words on the Wind

A collection of poems for every season of the soul

By

John and Laura Caldwell

DEDICATION

To our sons, Ethan and Caleb. Our love for you both is beyond measure, yet is nothing by comparison to the love of God for you both. May *His* Words on the Wind always lead you, guide you and bring you hope throughout your lives.

Yet this I call to mind
and therefore I have hope:
Because of the Lord's great love we are not consumed,
for his compassions never fail. They are new every morning;
great is your faithfulness.
I say to myself, "The Lord is my portion;
therefore I will wait for him."
The Lord is good to those whose hope is in him,
to the one who seeks him.

Lamentations 3:21-25

Contents

Introduction (John)

'Want to write a joint-book of poems?'

When I first raised the idea with Laura, I already had a title, a book cover, and a vague idea about the length of the book – about 70 pages.

Since Laura came on board, we've changed the title, the book cover, and a tsunami of poems from Laura all worked together to transform my rough concept into the finished project that you hold in your hands – God gives us wives to enhance us and enrich us in every way.

This project has been good for our own souls too. Both of us, independently, have been writing, journaling, and penning poems since we became Christians. Laura— a more consistent and prolific poet, and writer than I am – has a large crate of journals that could sink a battle-ship. Me? I had half-a-dozen journals and notepads, (scattered here, there and everywhere) that were made up of diary entries, reflections, and a few poems.

As we waded through our old journals, we were encouraged, and sometimes challenged by our own words from the past. So much of what we wrote in previous seasons seem relevant for our current season. Like-wise, a number of the more prophetic writings encouraged us because they predicted things that had come to pass.

As this project has taken shape, it has given us fresh encouragement from God. Seasons come and go – but God remains faithful.

As you encounter our seasons in each poem, may you find that these Words on the Wind breathe fresh encouragement, hope and strength as you discover Christ in the midst of your own season.

Introduction (Laura)

There is a scripture in Job 6:26 where it says "do you think you can reprove words when the speech of a despairing man is wind?"

There are times and seasons we go through in life, when like Job, we despair greatly. We long for a reason, a purpose in the trial. If our trial continues for a prolonged period of time, we can, like Job, have well-meaning friends who may try to assess the situation and, like Job's friends, get it wrong. Friends just want to help remedy the situation and cease your pain but, sometimes it can be to no avail.

Sometimes we can speak words out of pain and despair, which may paint a dark picture, one without hope. It can be hard for family or friend to listen without bringing reproof but the words of a despairing person are wind. To paraphrase John Piper: *to reprove that which is wind, gone with a change of circumstance may be futile. The darkness lifts and the bleak snapshot of that moment, that event, or even the dark night of the soul has ended –* words on the wind.

Words are like the autumn leaves, once securely fastened to the tree but the season changes and leaf loosens but oh the colours as it makes its departure – the leaves reveal to us there is beauty in letting go.

As the old saying goes, "better oot than in", and so, I often write in the varying seasons of the soul and the poems are often coupled with my words – expressing my woes, and God's word - lifting our eyes. I have in the past put some of my poems 'out there' and had so many more that have never seen the light of day. When John asked me if I wanted to do a book of poetry together I happily agreed. If anything written helps but one person then it has all been worth it. Jesus did not promise an easy life, but he did promise an eternal one.

So we do not lose heart. Though our outer self is wasting away, our inner self is being renewed day by day. For this light momentary affliction is preparing for us an eternal weight of glory beyond all comparison, as we look not to the things that are seen but to the things that are unseen. For the things that are seen are transient but the things that are unseen are eternal. 2 Corinthians 4:16

Seasons

John Caldwell

Like summer and winter, and autumn and spring,
Our life is a cycle of contrasting seasons,
There are times of distress, and times when we sing,
Yet through it all – good and bad – God has His reasons.

Heaven has its wise and perfect reasons,
Why you and I go through our seasons,
Of good and ill; laughter and sadness,
Our God brings good, out of every badness.

Life can be dark, harsh, and raging, like fierce winter storms,
The Lord moves mysteriously, His wonders He performs,
Our days can be bright and light, as joyful as summer sights,
Our God's at work, in the storm. In the rain. In the dark winter
nights.

God has His purpose, nothing happens without His reasons,
He's working out His plans, by taking you through seasons,
Each season we face, reveals His grace, and love and power,
The breaking of dawn always follows dusk's darkest hour.

So, take courage dear child of God, and trust in your Lord,
Though seasons shift and change, you must rely on His word,
When in a seasonal shift, your world can feel so strange,
But though the seasons alter, God's love will never change.

16.10.2018

The Gardener

Laura Caldwell

Don't fail to see the Gardener at work within your life
Don't fail to see His hand at work, when you feel the pruning knife
Don't fail to see the seasons that seem so very bare
Don't fail to know the Gardener's presence, for He is always there

Don't fail to see the Gardener, when the soil is being tilled
Don't fail to feel His tender touch, when the ditches are being filled
Don't fail to see the rocks, that seem so very big
Don't fail to know the Gardener's pruning of that not so fruitful
twig.

Don't fail to see the Gardener, when your life seems frozen over
Don't fail to know He's prepared the ground, and seeds planted
are well covered
Don't fail to know the season for the seed is not quite yet
Don't fail to recognise the harshness of conditions, be patient, do
not fret.

Don't fail to wait upon the time, that the Gardener has made
Don't fail to remind yourself during dearth, of the promises He said
Don't fail to be patient, knowing that in due time, your fruit shall
burst right out
Don't fail to encourage yourself and believe when assailed with
fear and doubt

Don't fail to come to the garden, to meet the Gardener there
Don't fail to remember He loves you, for you He truly cares
Don't fail to see the Gardener' s hand, at work in every place
Don't fail to know the Gardener's presence, for in His heart you
have a place

2010

In-between

Laura Caldwell

I find myself in-between, where I'm going and where I've been

I don't know what the path is, I only know You're with me

For here You are, by my side, taking rest on this stormy ride

For You know the plan, and You know the way

You only ask I take Your hand, and believe in what you say

Only believe, let faith arise

Only believe, let faith arise

And give it wings to fly

09.2006

Poetry

John Caldwell

Poetry: the language of the heart,

when deep in woes,

Poetry: the expression of the soul,

when joy overflows.

Poetry: more unreliable, and erratic, and unpredictable,

than the wind that blows,

Poetry: Unruly! Rebellious!

Less conventional than prose.

Poetry: the song for every high,

and the lament for all our lows.

Poetry: a pastor, a priest, and a prophet,

balm for the wounded, a sword against foes.

Poetry: the language of the soul, when words fail,

and comforts flee – Poetry knows.

3.08.2018

The night the power cut off

Laura Caldwell

It had been a difficult night, I had broke.
The heartache that had gripped me, the struggle of faith and
belief.
The inability to see, to understand.
The fear of returning to a place so dark, a life of separation,
loss of intimacy.
I could not go there.

That same night before I returned home, alongside came those
with strength:
To encourage, to lift my weary arms, to hold me as my knees
buckled.
As I poured out the depths of my being, the pain of loss,
The overwhelming emptiness.
Words of comfort were spoken, words of strength restored me.

I was not on a high, but in a place of fact.
Despite what the circumstances say, I will hold on.
Even when I cannot believe, just knowing God spoke it,
It will come to be.
Tired and weary, I lay down my head...
Exhausted.

I dreamt such vivid images, such piercing sounds.
As I was pulled from the place of sleep,
The piercing sound was a reality.
I struggled to register.
Was it within or without?
As I lay quietly listening, it became apparent,
It was within!
I had to arise.

I tried the light switch.
The light came on but it was so dim.
I tried the power socket but faded lights appeared.
Everything seems to be pale and weak.
I feared the fridge fault was the cause.
I should have had it addressed.
I sat on the bed...
Should I wait until morning? Should I call an electrician now?

It was 1.45 in the morning, what could be done?
Clarity struck through. Check all the house.
So I took a torch in hand, wandered downstairs,
It was the same everywhere, lights at half power.
Appliances pale and not enough power.
I switched them all off.

I returned to the fuse box.
I threw the switch...off...on.
No power at all now.
All was darkness.
Even the pale light had gone – what would I do?
A thought occurred – "is it just me?"
I looked outside to the darkness,
I could not tell.

I looked out the number, the one for emergencies.
I felt daft but I had to know.
"Good morning, Scottish Power Emergency line"
I gave my information,
"I'm not sure if it's just me or everyone"
She sounded so awake, considering the time,
"keep everything off but one light – just so you know when the
power comes back on."

Essential maintenance.

I breathed a sigh of relief – it wasn't just me.
How often do we question ourselves?
There are times when the power has to go off.
There are times when we need to be still in the darkness,
Not always knowing what is going on,
But knowing that God knows.

There are times essential maintenance has to be carried out in our
lives
Otherwise our power is at half, pale and weak,
Unable to power the smallest of appliances.

I lay there and understood, as it made a difference to hear,
"essential maintenance…whole area.."
So too, earlier in the evening, it had made a difference to hear,
"it's happening with everyone just now…"
And as I lay down to sleep after my call,
So I put to rest my conversation.
There is nothing I can do until the work is done so why lie awake.

I thank my Father for essential maintenance.
I thank my Father that though weeping may endure for a night,
Joy comes in the morning.
I thank God that the lights will come back on,
The power will return in full, no more pale and weak,
But full and strong.
I thank my Father that I had learned earlier in the evening, a lesson
that I put to use only hours later,
Don't panic in the darkness thinking "it's just me"

Switch everything off,
Lie and rest,
But leave one light on,
Just so you know when the power is back on.

2006

This is a season

Laura Caldwell

This is a season in your life
Live and walk through this season
Knowing and believing
The best is yet to be
Do not rely upon human logic
But rely upon God's word
Maintain an assured hope for the future
And do not cast away your confidence in Him
Nor cast away your confidence in His promises
In the midst of this great trouble
He is with you, He always has been
And always will be
Hold on dear one, hold on.

Keep on believing
You are not forgotten
You have not slipped His mind
Your name is written on His hand
Do not give up!
Take a rest with Him
This is a journey you are doing together
Don't trust in your own strength but in God's strength
This is not a dead-end situation, it's not the end of the road
He is Your heavenly Father, you can call on Him
Stand upon His word and promises
In faith
You have a future
Expect and watch things turn around
Trust in God, He is the One who can do it for you.

2005

Words on the Wind

John Caldwell

Bruised and broken, hope almost binned,
Lying face down as the enemy grinned,
Dressed in dirty clothes, I knew I had sinned,
Yet your grace came, like words on the wind.

Like a gentle, warm breeze, I feel your embrace,
Your words on the wind, blow away my disgrace,
You dispel the dark clouds, I see the sun's rays.
You invite me once more, to walk in your ways.

The words on the wind, bring me fresh hope,
The words breathe strength, when I cannot cope,
The wind of the Spirit, brings a word from the Lord,
As I lie here bleeding, having fallen on my sword.
The words on the wind, like a magic-potion,
Pour oil on my wound, like a healing lotion.
The words on the wind are words of healing,
This stone-cold heart once again is feeling,
Your nearness, your touch, your mighty power,
I rise to my feet, I look, I see the enemy cower.
His grinning countenance has turned to fear,
He intended to separate, but he's brought you near.
His tricks never change, he comes with temptation,
And as soon you bite, he starts his accusation –

"Call yourself a Child of God?"
"You're nothing but a hypocrite!"
"You're on the road that's broad"
"your destiny's the burning pit!"
"There is no more that you can do!"
"You've gone too far, he's finished with you!"

This is the devil's tactic, it works time and time again,
And were it not, for the words on the wind,
We'd never rise, we'd be out the game.
Down and out, never to rise, forever haunted by shadows of
shame –
But the words on the wind come to rekindle, the flickering, feeble,
dying flame.

There comes a time when the child of God,
feels they've failed the test,
Let these words on the wind come to you
and carry you to his rest.
Battle weary, tested to the limit,
and carrying guilt like cosmic treason,
His words on the wind come to us,
with a word for every season –
The words on the wind rush from heaven,
to help the weary-hearted,
Whispering hope:
"God's plan for you is not over.
It's barely even started!"

13.10.2018

Step beyond the boundary

Laura Caldwell

I stood at the fence, the bolt was secure
so early in the morning, yet no more sleep could I endure
and so it was I arose, and made a cup of tea
wandered to the garden's edge and looked out to see
the loch it was so peaceful, the birds sang sweetly in the trees
and the thought just filled my mind, I am truly free
for there I stood in the open, with my PJs and my fleece
a cup of tea in hand, and boots up to my knees
and I stood in awe, as I watched the water glide
like oil on a surface, the smooth flow of morning tide
the burn could be heard, making its way down mountainside
dashing over stones and pebbles, like the hero to his bride
I watched where it flowed, beneath the bridge of stone
it had joined the loch and no longer flowed alone
it was then I noticed, the mooring and the boat
and straight away, into my head, came this little thought
I was like that little boat, I thought I was at sea
floating on the water, surrounded by such beauty
thinking I was living, when life was passing me by
for I was tied to a mooring but within me was a cry
I knew that there was more for me, I just did not know what
I wanted to go out further but to the mooring I was caught
now this mooring, it has good, for in the storm it holds fast
but there comes a time in life that you need to cast
the things that keep you back, in a place of fear
throw off these things that hinder and keep your mind clear
just undo the rope and push out from the shore
and take the oars and row, for there is so much more

I saw in that moment, that I still held back
standing at this fence, some courage I did lack
to venture beyond this point, for fear of being seen

so I threw it off, and determined to change this fearful gene
I pulled back the bolt and opened the gate wide
cup of tea in hand, I took a step outside
I closed the gate behind me and walked down to the shore
for I saw so clearly, there was so much more
the boat it was so beautiful, a lovely sight to view
but when gliding through the waves, going to waters new
the purpose that is found, the excitement of 'setting sail'
is worth far more than comfort or fears that you may fail
for failure is allowed, we learn from the things we do
as long as we don't give up, but keep on pressing through
what is it keeps you fenced, behind that bolted gate?
that keeps you from launching from the shore, telling you it's too late
I sat that morning for an hour, watching time go by
I felt so at peace and free, I simply let out a sigh
seeing that I cannot see, what the future will hold
I can only walk a step at a time and watch it all unfold
Later that day, an offer was made to me
would I stay upon the shore or take the boat out to the sea?
My initial response was stay, to remain upon the land
but, when I thought to myself, 'to set sail would be so grand'
so welly boots and waterproofs upon myself were dressed
and as we rowed out from the shore I considered myself blessed
for I learned on the journey how to handle an oar
how to guide an engine until my arm was sore
I saw my surroundings from a whole new perspective
and the time I spent out there, made me so reflective

It's pretty to stand upon the edge and look out from the shore
but it's so amazing when you sail out - you see so much more
and so from this I've learned, not to stay behind the gate
but take the risk and push on out, who knows what excitement
awaits...

2006

23

Chosen by Grace

John Caldwell

Is it possible? Can it be true?
That it wasn't my choice, to be chosen by you?
If it is possible, how can it be?
Despite my rebellion, you chose to call me?

A sinner at heart, no good of my own,
Saved only by grace, through faith alone.

My Father, can it be true?
That *I* am chosen by *you*?

Nothing on my part, not even my will,
Could ever, no never, your law fulfil.
Not even your requirement, to 'only believe',
Can be grasped by a sinner – who cannot receive!

As a blind man cannot give himself sight,
As the darkness cannot turn into light,
As the dead man cannot bring himself out the grave,
Only a sovereign God, can sovereignly save!

My will is corrupt, prone only to stray,
It's you alone who leads me your way.
Should I ever think, I must keep myself right,
I soon realise, that I can't win this fight.

In the heat of temptation. In the darkest hour.
I can only depend, on your keeping power!

05.11.2007

Two black polo necks

Laura Caldwell

Two black polo necks have I
'a polo neck is a polo neck' I hear you cry
But although they may appear to be similar
There is difference in the detail with which I am familiar
One is more suited to wear with jeans
And the difference between them surely means
That the purpose of each is so unique
To wear one instead of the other would be weak

And so it is in this world and our life
We are unique and cause ourselves such strife
Aiming to please others and trying to be something
Instead of being who we are and just relaxing
Others maybe appear to have it all
Singing and dancing and having a ball
Could it be that they have discovered who they are
Or could it be they hide inside, keeping thoughts afar

Take time out to speak to your Creator
For He knows you intimately, do it now, not later
He alone, can tell you – your worth
For He planned for you before your birth
The gifts you would have and the gap you would fill
He has determined but you have the will
To choose to discover the life, the plan
Or wander aimlessly trying to please man.

Or maybe you have dreams, within your heart and mind
Of things you long for, but just cannot find
This life falls short of your expectations
And disappointments and failure display your limitations

Take time out to speak to your Creator
I urge you do it soon, and not later
For only He can meet you in the place that you stand
And restore your life and take your hand

There are things in life, we think will make us happy
It's just not true, that philosophy is crappy
For happiness is not found in things external
But peace and joy is a foundation internal
And I have discovered this gift in my Creator
Life forced me to do it, now, and not later
And I am so glad that God took the time
To break into, this life of mine
For I have learned, that His love is beyond measure
He's held me close, and told me I'm His treasure
My foundations in this life had been so broken
But words of strength and peace, into my life He's spoken

Things are so simple now, life is for living
Being content, at peace and forgiving
For in the circumstances I faced, I expected to die
Instead I learned of God, how to live, it's no lie

People may appear to have similar gifts as each other but none can fit so perfectly in a situation where another should be. For it's in the fine detail that God blows people away. So don't worry if others have similarities. Or that you'll be discarded.
For you are unique, as is your purpose. Be ready to be that word, for that time, when God will blow someone away with the fine detail of your life.

2006

I started on this journey

Laura Caldwell

I started on this journey

A long time ago

And where this path would lead me

I just didn't know

I'd lived my life as I wanted to

Going my own way

Until I met with Jesus

In a very special way

He gave me love

Like I had never known

Wrapped me in His loving arms

And called me to His own

He gave me a new life

And a reason to go on

Filled my life with meaning

And put within my heart a song

2006

The Enemy's Accusation

John Caldwell

Tired and weary, I wander on through,

Continually asking 'what should I do?'

The battle rages on every side,

Guilt, fear and shame, cause my feet to slide.

Temptations within, trials without,

Day and night, I hear the enemy shout.

Losing sight of my purpose, I can't see my goal,

I struggle to keep myself out of this hole,

No strength to continue, like one who is lame,

I barely have the power to call on your name.

Your grace, your joy, your peace, I need,

Only speak the Word and I shall be freed!

Your Word and your cross, my only hope.

Why do I give the enemy so much scope?

Though my flesh prevails, and though I fail,

Once more your grace will enable me to sail.

05.11.2007

The older brother - am I?

Laura Caldwell

I am not like that brother of mine
I've stayed pure, no pig slime.
Stayed within the confines of the family place
I've not gone off without a trace.
Worked so hard for my father at home,
I've not taken off, the world to roam,
I am not like that brother of mine.

I am not like that brother of mine,
Taken his money before it's time.
Our inheritance was due much later,
That brother of mine is such a traitor.
Wild living and partying hard,
Oh brother - I have marked your card,
I am not like that brother of mine.

I am not like that brother of mine,
I take pride in our family line.
Never taking time out of service to dad,
I'm the good guy, my brother is bad.
It's alright for him to go off,
Living and feeding from a trough,
I'm not like that brother of mine.

I am not like that brother of mine,
He's been away such a long time.
Where did he go? Am I my brother's keeper?
Left here to serve, while in sin he goes deeper.

Is he alive? Do I care?
Why should I, he's taken his share!
I'm not like that brother of mine!

I am not like that brother of mine,
He belongs with those swine!
Living in filth, a pig sty is right,
That's where he should stay, out of my sight!
Here am I, righteous and faithful,
Not like that sinning creature who's hateful.
I am not like that brother of mine.

Look at me, hard-working and serving,
I am so much more deserving.
Thinking much of myself, I stand tall,
I am clean, and I do not crawl.
I've stayed true, I am no sinner,
I've never even had a fatted calf dinner!

Here I am, look at me!
A pure bred, fine serving, specimen, that's me!
That brother of mine— hang on! Is that him I see?
Oh, he better forget coming anywhere near home,
He had his chance and he chose to roam.
He made his bed, he can lie in it for sure,
That turncoat sibling is far from pure!
How dare he show his face back here!

This place is mine, I've worked for it alone,
You've had your share, now go, be gone!
Look at him! Filthy starver - get out of here!
Don't you dare come anywhere near.

What is dad doing? Dad?? Stop! Wait!
Why are you running out through the gate?
You've got to be kidding me? I cannot believe!
Dad! Are you mad? Don't you see me?
Argh! Dad let him go, you don't know where he's been
Look at him, he's filthy, he's unclean.

What??? The ring, the robe, and now the calf!
Now you're really having a laugh!
Dad, I am here, your faithful son,
I am your boy, your only one!

All this time I've worked hard for you,
Have you got a ring, robe and calf for me too?
You're throwing HIM a party - what about me?
I stayed home - don't you see?
You're celebrating him? I just don't get it,
He's off partying and I'm here sweating it!
He saunters home after who knows how long,
And you go hug him?! Now a Feast and a song?
Dad, what about me? I've been here all the time
I am not like that brother of mine!

My son, you've been here all along,
You could have had a feast, a robe, a song!
But this brother of yours was thought to be dead.
But here he is alive, and my heart has no dread.
For my son has come home, your brother is well!
He has learned a lesson and learned it well.
You my child, need to look at your heart,
For it is wicked, it is dark.
You may have stayed home and done all that is 'right',
But your heart is dark, it lacks the light
Open your eyes and look and see,
You have the spirit of a Pharisee

The lessons are many to be learned from this,
Your standing in glory is dependent on Jesus.
The sinner has a place at the foot of the cross,
Thinking not of yourself more than you ought.
To those who believe and cry "Jesus forgive me"
Will forgiveness be given and they'll be set free.

But to the older brother, let this truth be seen,
Your righteousness is filthy, you are unclean.
Perfect living and esteem of man,
Cannot deliver you out of my hand.

With judgement I'm coming, and of this there's no doubt,
The facade of your life and true heart will be found out.
May the scales fall from your eyes and lay down your pride,
And to the foot of the cross run with all your might.
For it is not your righteousness or good deeds that you've done,
But in Christ alone that your sins are atoned.

07.09.2018

Judgement day

Laura Caldwell

When you stand before the King on that judgement day

What will you have to bring Him? What is it that you'll say?

Will you provide a list of service, or show your works at length?

Declaring gifts you've given and how you tithed a tenth?

When your book of life is opened, and the judgement is

pronounced

Will you be a faithful servant or will you be denounced?

I want to be sure, that I'll spend eternity

In the presence of my Saviour, for He has died for me

He's the only One that matters, His blood has paid my price

There's nothing I can offer but my life

If you think that you are worthy, because you have been good

My friend you are mistaken, you've not really understood

When I read the bible and think on what it says

A man is justified not by works or by how he prays

Galatians 2:16 says, it's through faith in Jesus Christ

We can come before the throne of God, because He paid the price

Have you made big sacrifices and feel that you can brag?

Don't you know dear friend your works are, all but filthy rags?

For we stand not in our goodness, but because we have believed

In Christ alone we're righteous, God's mercy we've received

We have been redeemed, not by the works of man

But by the precious blood of Jesus – God's redemption plan

Jesus, only Jesus, He is ever interceding

He is my righteousness

Jesus, only Jesus, Lamb of God and Saviour

The way, the truth, the life.

22.02.2011 (song)

Perfect Living

Laura Caldwell

I used to think I had to live a perfect life
As in Proverbs 31, I was that dutiful wife
Finding my worth in the roles that I played
It was no wonder I became dismayed
For failure was not an option for me
Bound by conditioning, I just couldn't see
Living a life, that was just an existence
But God broke through with His persistence
For His word says we are to have a life
Abundant and full, although not free from strife
And so when things went wrong, as often they do
I thought I was being punished, it just wasn't true
But such was my thinking, my mindset, my ways
I tried to be perfect, but was sad and afraid
Trapped in a prison of emotions and doubt
Until God came, to show the way out
I was so afraid to make a mistake
Any show of weakness caused me to break
I felt I had to be strong and never falter
And my way of living this did halter
Living for others in the hope I'd be accepted
Living in fear of being rejected
Finding it hard to ever truly trust
Not really knowing love, only lust
Trying to please those all around
Only drove me deeper into the ground
But thankfully God cares so much for me
He didn't leave me in that place, but set me free
Breaking down barriers I'd built to guard
Removing boulders from my life and softening my heart

I hadn't realised the depths that this went
and many broken hours of weeping I spent
as it dawned on me, a victim I'd been
of all that my life was, I had never seen
as difficult as it was, to face these things
the lessons I learned, the peace it brings
my worth is no longer tied to any role
in this area I believe I'm now whole
no longer living for man's acceptance or love
and for this liberty I thank God above
stripped of all I thought I knew
not knowing if, or how I'd get through
for there were days I thought I'd die
but in it all God's taught me to rely
upon His love for He'll never leave
and comfort He brings to those who grieve
"why does He allow suffering? If such a God of care"
Exact answers I know not, but my thoughts I'll share
He has given man a will that is free
Decisions and choices can be made easily
God will not force us into His way
But will guide us when we begin to stray
Are our ears open to hear His word?
Are our eyes seeing or is our vision blurred?
I have learned of God in these recent years
Learned of His love as He's wiped away tears
This love He has for us, all thinking defies
Will you believe truth or the master of lies?
For there is an enemy who seeks to end
Our lives in all ways, on this you can depend
That our destruction, is what he seeks
And has no conscience of the deceit he speaks
For his end is decided and he has nothing to lose
But you have, so I ask, what will you choose?
A life of freedom in the God of creation
For He has paid for your salvation

Making a way through His son on the cross
Who considered not Himself as loss
But cried out, "it is done"
The price for all was paid by One
For such is my love for you
There is nothing I would not do
You are Mine, if you'd only see
I want you with me, for eternity
I dare you to seek the giver of life
And I promise it won't be free from strife
But strength you will find and amazing love
As God opens the windows of heaven above
And pours out His blessings on you each day
You'll be overwhelmed if you chose this way

2006 (latter part of this poem is part of a song I wrote called Remember Me).

Look beyond the face

Laura Caldwell

There is a sadness that fills my heart

When people can be so cruel

They judge so quickly a person's demise

And consider them a fool

This person's life may not have been so easy

They may have not had the same opportunity

And yet you consider nothing but the cover

From your judgements there's no impunity

If only you could see the heart within

Breaking, yet its sorrow is heard with a laugh

The life that is before you is a mirage

If you only knew the half

Maybe you wouldn't be so quick

To condemn and write off with no hope

Maybe you would take the time

To learn to see how they cope

To today I ask you, have some compassion

Put yourself within their place

Don't always go by the 'front' that is shown

But look beyond the face

2.11.2006

I Can Pray

John Caldwell

When all else fails.
I can pray.
When hope departs.
I can pray.
If I fail.
I can pray.
If I think I won't make it.
I can pray.
While I have breath.
I can pray.

Lord, grant me the desire to pray.

21.11.2007

On the edge

Laura Caldwell

I stand on the edge, excitement and terror run side by side
And I get buckled in for this unknown rollercoaster ride
I cannot see the route, I only see the start
My palms are clammy, and there's quick rhythm to my heart
My breathing is not flowing, but coming in a short and shallow way
As fear and trepidation build within me, as I face this day

I had stood at a distance, so often in the past
Watching others enjoy the ride, and truly having a blast
I had so wanted to join them, but fear held me to the spot
I never made the most of the 'all rides ticket' I had bought
I wasn't disappointed, or even a bit disconcerted
For I accepted the decisions made, but then something happened I
had not expected.

My life was torn apart, from the outside in
And it made me stop and look, at this life that I was living
A life of fear and compromise, a life in a comfort zone
Until the bombshell dropped and suddenly my cover was blown.

For I thought that it was right, to hide it all away
But now I have learned to live, and face life come what may
And so I joined the queue, at the rollercoaster ride
Terrified but determined, with friends right by my side
As I buckled in, and down the harness came
I knew from that moment, my life would never be the same
There was no turning back, no way for me to escape
So I gripped on tightly, my eyes and mouth agape.

It started oh so slowly, making its ascent
And I was absolutely terrified, as up to the top we went.
The view was so amazing, but my heart was in my mouth
When the carriage dropped so suddenly, and I screamed out loud
"m-a-a-a-m-m-m-i-e-e-e-e", all the way I cried
I just couldn't stop, no matter how I tried.

As fast as it had started, so it came to an end
All those twists and turns, ups and downs and bends.
The adrenalin had kicked in, and the terror replaced with high
As I stepped out from the carriage, and let out a great big sigh
I had finally done it, the fear of the ride was gone
I felt so exhilarated, and my face and eyes just shone.

And so it is, I have discovered, in this life of mine
There are many journeys to make, and mountains to climb
It may appear so immense, and fear attempt to restrain
But I'm learning to throw it off, and my mind re-train
For I am loved of God, I'm His daughter and His child
And He has made me as I am, varying from mild to wild.

I live my life learning, and growing from all I see
But best of all I've learned, to be content with 'me'.
Not trying to be someone else, or gain people's affection
Learning to love and forgive, and no longer fear rejection
I once thought I was unlovable, and I believed the lie
But now I know otherwise, I am loved by God Most High

2006

Freedom

Laura Caldwell

Bound by all I thought I should be
The things of life they fashioned me
The people around me and the opinion of man
Kept me in chains, and out of Your plan
There came a day when You drew me aside
To show me in You, I could confide
My deepest pains, my darkest sorrow
The guilt of yesterday and fears for tomorrow
Freedom in the place You're taking me to
Free to be me, created by You
Free to laugh
Free to sing
Free to dance
My praise I'll bring
For You are making me free

2006

The Blood that bids me come

John Caldwell

Lord, I thank you for the precious blood.

The blood that bids me come.

No matter how often I fail —

You bid me come.

You offer me:

Hope —

like the sun's rays,

Piercing

through threateningly fierce, black, stormy clouds.

Mercy —

like rain after a summer drought.

Forgiveness —

like a feast after a famine.

21.11.2007

Thank You

Laura Caldwell

Thank You for Your strength, Thank You for Your care
Thank You for believing and always being there

Thank You for Your faithfulness, Thank You for Your truth
Thank You for Your love that never can be moved

For in the time of deepest sorrow, You never left my side
And in the times of trouble, You gave me place to hide
And even in the darkness, when I could face no more
You came into my life and opened up the door

Thank You for Your mercy, Thank You for Your grace
Thank You for Your wisdom, that gave me strength to face

Thank You for believing, Thank You for Your love
Thank You for Your faith, that You showered from above

And now I see that all's not easy, like gold refined by fire
You're bringing forth Your champions, for Your ways are higher

When we can find no purpose, in the trouble that we see
I hear Your voice calling, "my child, just believe"

01.2005

The Lion's Roar

John Caldwell

Can you hear the Lion's roar?
It calls the church, once more to soar,
To rise up from the ashes of defeat,
To come before the Mercy Seat,
To leave behind shame and disgrace,
To get on her knees and seek His face.

There is a coming, mighty tide,
The King comes looking for his Bride,
With waves of mercy, waves of grace,
Spot or wrinkle, there can be no trace.
As she gets herself clean, and makes herself holy,
She prepares herself for the coming glory.

And as it was at Pentecost,
The Lord shall usher in the lost,
Tongues of fire – a rushing wind,
Now clothed in white are those who once sinned.

With a sword in their hands, and a fire in their hearts,
Their faith, a shield, from the enemy's darts,
All opposition, they take in their stride,
As God raises up his Warrior Bride.
With consciences cleansed and hearts washed pure,
In a sin-sick world, they bring God's cure.

With banners raised high, they march ahead,
Preaching the gospel and raising the dead.
Awakening sinners, restoring lost sheep,
Those who are slumbering, arise from their sleep.
Cripples are healed, and prisoners set free,
The deaf will hear, the blind will see.

They cast out demons, they speak with new power,
They reflect God's glory, it's the final hour.
They fulfil the commission, empowered from on high,
For this cause, they will live or die.
Their hearts they long, for the return of the King,
As the Day approaches, this new song they sing:

You've opened our eyes, you've broken our chains,
You've healed our hearts, you've washed our stains,
We now lay aside all earthly gain,
You are the Lamb, for us you were slain!

Run with this vision, let hope remain,
The Lord will pour out the latter rain,
Be ever prepared, get into place,
Trust not in yourself, but only his grace.
Know your Lord, yourself, and know your mission;
Keep in your hearts this latter-day vision.
For the time has come, his church to restore,
Listen! Can you hear it? The Lion's Roar!

21.11.2007

Warrior child

Laura Caldwell

Arise my warrior child, arise, my warrior bride
For it's almost time for you to come and be by my side
A champion of the King, an overcomer are you
For I will never leave you and I will bring you through.

The enemy has come with his lies and his deceit
Telling you I've left you, and that you will be beat
LISTEN TO ME NOW and listen to me well
I WILL NEVER leave you and this is how you'll tell
Listen in the midst, of the chaos that does surround
Take the time in silence and soon I will be found
For as you come to seek Me, in the midst of all
Be sure my daughter, my son, I will come near when you call

For my plans for you are good, but you have no need to fear
For you are in my hand and I AM always near
It may seem that I am distant, but this is just not true
I am but in the background, keeping my eye on you
For time I have held back, and silent I have been
For the testing of your heart and to show all that is unseen
To expose all the weakness, so that you might be strong
Be sure my son, my daughter, my return won't be very long

Be prepared and just be ready, for over you I will roar
The Lion of Judah is coming, you won't need to weep any more
For over you He stands, to protect and to guard
For the enemy has sought to destroy you, and take away your
heart
But the Master, He has kept it, in a place of safety and of rest
And soon He will return it to you, but by Him it has been blessed
A heart of love and passion, a heart steadfast and true
A heart for the Father's heart, a heart of love for you

A time of blessing awaits you, a time of provision and supply
Watch as I open the windows of heaven, look up and watch the sky
For in it you will see, signs of the coming time
Behold I stand before you, put your hand in Mine
Together we'll make this journey, and I say to you 'be strong'
Do not fear the battle, or fear you've got it wrong
For strategies will be revealed to you, and ways to bring an end
To the bondages of those around you, and to unlock the hearts of
men.

For the time is very near, my return is so very soon.
But there is yet a work to do, the child is yet in the womb
For this generation will rise, not seeking its own success
But will walk in honour and in integrity, and they will be blessed
For they will seek the Giver, they will seek the Father's heart
They seek to dwell in My presence, and do not wish to depart

My heart, it swells, for this is the very reason
That the hearts of men and women, would find me in this season
They will not be won by fancy words, or dramatic displays
But those who walk with Me, and show forth my ways
A way not of religion, not of form, no regulations or rule
But a way of life so simple, you may be regarded as fools
But it is the foolish things, of this earth that I intend to use
I'm coming, I'm coming, I'm coming to light the fuse
The fuse to spark revival, revival to light the flame
Once lit within a life, it shall never be the same

Can you hear Me coming? Can you hear the lion roar?
The Lion of Judah is returning, and you will weep no more!
Lift up your heads, look up. Look up and watch the sky,
For your night is over, look up, your morning is drawing nigh,
Weeping has endured, but its time now at an end
Learn well and live, and on Me only depend
For this is that time, for which you've been prepared
Do not think yourself unable, and do not be scared

For I will give you everything, you need to walk with Me
Keep your eyes focused, and I will let you see
The wonders of the heavens, insight into lives of men
Listen and I'll give you words, to speak and to pen
Words of wisdom and discernment, words of courage and of hope
Words of life for those around, that will give them cause to cope
And in the midst of the calling, as you walk in all I request
Be sure that I am with you, and know that you will be blessed

12.12.2007

Long has been this path

Laura Caldwell

Long has been this path and hard has been this road
This journey of discovery, that many feet have trod
Discovering you in the midst of this trial
Discovering me and the fight for survival
I wouldn't wish this pain upon any other
And yet I feel Your protection and I sense Your cover
My Father and my guide, to You I ask this day
Please take me by the hand and lead me on Your way
For my heart within is breaking and I can't face alone
This path of pain and grief that causes me to groan
Please come and be my strength, my very strong tower
And where my strength is gone, fill me with your power
That there will come a day of freedom and of rest
When I will stand strong and I will be dressed
With the garments of salvation and sing a song of praise
For though I fell and wept, I once again was raised
For the enemy didn't realise that when he crushed me down
You would lift me up and place upon my head a crown
his plan for me was harm, but Yours for me was good
And when this battle's o'er, he'll wish he'd understood
A life within God's hand is a force with which to be reckoned
Do not walk away when you hear Him, to you beckon
For God will be your rampart, your fortress and your guide
He will lead you safely and never leave your side
His heart is always for you, He made you, you're His child
His love is ever toward you, it cannot be reviled
And so this day be strong and do not stop the race
For when you finish here, in heaven you have a place

2006

Getting better

Laura Caldwell

I know I'm getting better,
I know I'm growing strong,
but there are days that still go slowly,
and times go on so long
The emotions still come and take me,
on a journey I've come to know,
but deep within my heart
I know You love me so
For You're my comfort, my rock,
my strength, my friend,
You will never leave me,
on You I can depend
And this I've learned so deeply,
and come to know of late,
for You have been my shelter, and kept my love from hate
You've changed my life so much,
that I can honestly say,
even though I don't understand,
I know You'll make a way
In what may seem impossible,
and when all around says "no",
because of what You've promised,
You will make it so
And so I want to say Thank You,
for giving my life new hope,
and filling my heart with strength
when I felt I couldn't cope
For in the days gone past,
I would've taken the easy way out,
but You've filled my life with meaning
and removed from me all doubt

For before I couldn't believe,
that I was worth the love,
but You've opened the windows of heaven
and showered me from above
You've replaced my fear with trust
and my insecurity with peace,
You've given me a reason
and caused my striving to cease
For my life, it is a gift
that You've given me,
I now give back to You
that I might be free
For it's in the letting go,
that gifts take on their role,
not holding them tightly to you,
for that strain takes its toll
Allow your gift the freedom,
the space in which to grow,
and watch how much more fruitful
and how your gift does grow

12.06.2005

Grace for failure

John Caldwell

Jesus I need you to work in my life,
Sin rages within, it causes me strife.
I long for your presence, I long for your touch,
I haven't been faithful, yet you've given me much.
Is it too late? Can I find my way back?
Will it be possible to get on track?

You died in my place.
Your blood pleads my case.

Your cross speaks favour.
Your cross speaks grace.
Your cross speaks mercy,
It's the Father's embrace.

It is Finished.
It is Finished.
Guilt be gone!
Fear be diminished!
Shame has no right.
It cannot stay.
For my Salvation.
God,
His Son,
Did slay.

21.11.2007

Discouraged

Laura Caldwell

It would seem that hope has been lost
People don't want to count the cost
It's all about 'me' and 'what I want'
'where is your God?', the enemy taunts
Faced with failure, and no fruit from sowing
It seems there's a desert where nothing is growing
The fields are empty, there's no grapes on the vine
The olive crop fails and men are blind
Fig trees have no blossoms, it all seems dead
Until the Bible I picked up and this I read
"the sovereign Lord, He is my strength" it says
"you have need of endurance in these days"
"hold on tight to the hope that you have"
For there will be days again when you will laugh
"keep your confident trust in God,
For with it will come a great reward"
I try to encourage myself and not give in
Trusting that God, will strengthen me within
So when discouraged, don't give up hope
But hold on to God, He WILL help you cope!

2006

Scotland's Scenes

John Caldwell

Miles of misty, mysterious hills,
The heart enlarges, the mind is stilled,
Scenic Scotland, the soul it thrills,
Its haunting landscape excites and chills.

Vast beaches, barren, blazing white sand,
Towering cliffs, so majestic and grand,
Forever on your soul, their image, they brand,
It is not difficult to understand,
Why many are drawn to Bonnie Scotland.

A peninsular postcard: picturesque,
A coastal cliff coaster, for your desk.
Spectacular scenes, a mountainous view,
But is this the only Scotland you knew?

Eclipsed by splendid, saintly scenes,
Lie Scotland's dark and hellish schemes,
Concrete jungles, an urban zoo,
This is the Scotland you never knew.

Tower blocks and run-down tenement flats,
Next-door neighbours, just nameless stats.
Community crumbling, individuals' reign,
'Survival of the fittest' is the name of the game.

While drug-dealers claim 'The American Dream',
Poverty, pain, powerlessness, mark the schemes,
Addiction, hopelessness, crime: the themes,
'Bonnie Scotland' aint so Bonnie, so it seems.

Fatherless families fight through their fears,
Young people drowning in drugs and beers,
Pop pills, numb the pain, and resist the tears,
A silent cry, which no one hears.

Emptiness: the inheritance, of this generation,
A hollow shell, this soulless nation.
A barren land; a waterless brook,
An empty Kirk; a forgotten book.
Be gone with your romantic Scottish vision!
The land lies dying, in need of mission.

2015 (First published in 'Christ, the Cross, and the Concrete Jungle')

When I'm here

Laura Caldwell

When I'm here and surrounded, by such amazing beauty
I wonder at how this world, can be filled with so much cruelty
But then I remember, that God gave man the choice
To stand and watch in silence, or take action and raise his voice
With every day that passes, opportunities arise
To see what's going on, or else divert our eyes
To be concerned with what we see and act accordingly
Or simply walk on by, because 'it's nothing to do with me'
How often do we stop?
Have we ever taken time?
To get to know the reason why
The beggar holds that sign
'hungry and homeless'
'please give me your spare change'
Or do we walk on past
Labelling them as deranged?
They too were born as we
A babe so small and calm
And life has made a path
That didn't shelter them from harm
Maybe they made choices
That were not so very wise
But who are we to judge?
But for God's grace go I.
So I lay aside my thoughts
And cares about this life
And just walk in the midst of majesty,
Forgetting this world's strife
If only for the moment,
In this place I find such rest
And thank my God above,
For I am truly blessed.
2006

Paradise Lost, and Restored

John Caldwell

Placed in the Garden of Paradise,
No pain, no death, no clinging vice,
No fears, no tears, no money arrears.

No depression, no stress,
No guilt to fight, or suppress.
No sleepless nights, no regrets,
No anxious thoughts, no debts.

Into the peaceful garden of Paradise,
Came a slippery snake, a devil in disguise,
A sparkling empty promise, a seductive appeal.
But you never win, when with the devil you deal.

The devil came, offering so much more,
But when you taste his fruit, it's rotten to the core,
A curse awakened, judgement falls,
The snake on its belly, forever it crawls.

Women in child-birth, deep pain will now know,
Man works for crops, but it's thorns that will grow.
Paradise gone. Hell spills over the earth,
Death is the destiny of those brought to birth,

But all is not lost, for a promise is given,
There will be a way, to recover heaven.
From the woman, a child will be born,
One who'll be pierced, by Adam's thorn,

The serpent's bite will inflict him pain,
The Son will die – but rise again.
And as his body receives new breath,
He'll rise victorious over death.
He'll pay the price to set us free,
He has the power, to help us see.
Will we receive His reviving breath?
The Spirit of Life, that conquers death!

The gates of paradise are swung open wide,
But will you enter? You must decide.
Will you come to Jesus and turn from your sin?
Will Heaven be yours, will you enter in?
Not everyone makes it, can't you tell?
Some choose sin, their destiny's hell.
Run while there's time, do not delay,
Trust Jesus alone, be restored today.

17.01.2014

Who holds the oceans

Laura Caldwell

Who holds the oceans in His palm
Or takes the sky in hand?
Who can lift the earth and weigh the mountains of this land?
Who can tell Him? Who could say?
Name one who taught God how to make a day.

The nations are so small
Beside His vast expanse
Islands are but dust, within His mighty hands.
Take the world and all it is
Life with Father God – there's nothing like this.
Nothing can compare
Nothing comes close
The creator of all things,
to you, new life He brings

Have you not seen? Have you not heard? Don't you understand?
It is God who formed the night sky and calls each star by name
He made us all unique, no two are quite the same.
You are His creation, unique in all you are
He has not forgotten you, He is not very far
His thoughts toward you never change, you're the reason Jesus
died
For it was not the nails that held Him but His love held Him fast, it
cannot be denied

Open your eyes to see, open your ears to hear
The Creator of all that you can see, is calling you to come near

14.06.2007

(Song based on Isaiah 40:12-17)

Pentecost

John Caldwell

Drops like a bomb on

enemy territory:

Day of Pentecost.

16.10.2018

Post-Pentecost

John Caldwell

The fire has died down, yet the people still gather, and haven't noticed that ice has set in.

14.07.2004

His hand

Laura Caldwell

It is His hand that fashions me

It is His hand that sets me free

It is His hope that lifts my heart

It is His faith that won't depart

For His hand is strong to hold me fast

For His love never ends and will always last

His hope in me causes me to soar

His faith opens before me even the closed door

Of whom do I speak? I hear you say

Who is this that you speak of in this way?

It is my God, my Saviour, my King

He is my all, my everything

His hand has lifted and carried me

His love fills my life for all to see

His hope has lifted me and my heart sings

His faith has given me eagle's wings

And so now I put my hand in His

I bow before my Father and feel His kiss

My hope in Him renews my sight

And by faith, all darkness will become light

2006

The child in me

Laura Caldwell

There is a child in me, that longs to be free
Father open this child's eyes, that the adult might see
Things are not so big, nor so very scary
There's no need to fear You, or reason to be wary
For all things that come, there is a cause
It all depends on reaction, so I take a pause
To consider before me, the path yet unknown
And consider the words, into my life You've sown
"for I know the plans", "good" and "prosperity"
"not for your harm", "a life of longevity"
Father I come, and I bring you my past
And lay it all before You, my burden I cast
I don't want to fear, its effect on my present
So I give it to You, that You will take the unpleasant
That the things gone before, will not affect my today
Nor my tomorrow, Father take it, I pray
That I will walk with honour, and courage, this path
For I know now, it was Your love and not wrath
That caused my life to so completely unravel
When I look at me now, I can only marvel
At the blessings poured out, and the gifts that were deep
Father, my Father, Your love makes me weep
I never imagined, my life could be so
So today I stand before You, I want You to know
I love You, I trust You, I believe in Your word
How could I doubt You, it seems so absurd
Thank You for everything, past, present, to come
Thank You, thank You for being the One.

22/01/2007

The Land of the Book? (Once Upon a Time . . .)
John Caldwell

In Scotland, Once upon a time,

The glory of the Son did shine,

The Celtic land did fall in love,

with religion, revealed from God above.

And so, the church and Scotland,

were together wed,

But love soon died,

and away Scotland went,

to another's bed.

And so, they've gone their separate ways,

Awaiting divorce, 'tis only a matter of days.

The Land of the Book is a myth of the past,

The national flag should fly at half-mast.

But instead of mourning, dancers take to the floor,

To celebrate the fact that the church rules no more.

The shackles are off, freedom is here,

'Each to their own' there's nothing to fear.

It's a new day, liberty dawns—

But are we kings? Or are we pawns?

Tolerance, freedom, inclusion the themes,

Buzz words masking totalitarian regimes.

Goodbye goodness. Goodbye truth,

Hello prison -- if you open your mouth.

"You have the right to remain silent,"

That you can keep.

"Free Speech" was stolen, as the church fell asleep.

It's time to wake up! It's time to pray.

That God, His hand of Judgement, might stay.

11. 01. 2014

Leave me not

Laura Caldwell

Leave me not alone this day

Come to my help, O Lord, I pray

For no more can I now endure

Of this, Lord, I am so sure

So hard and painful has been this path

Sometimes I wonder is it love or wrath,

That allows these tests to carry on?

Please God I pray, let them be gone

That I could find comfort and peace once more

And joy and delight at what you have in store

Please Lord I pray give me a break, this I ask for my own sake.

2006

The rhythm of life

Laura Caldwell

It is only God who can meet our deepest need
It is only God who can see into the deepest places of our hearts
We try in vain to hide the ugly things we see, we try in vain to hide
what we are
But know this, God already sees, God already knows
And yet His love for us still stands.
He is not thwarted by the flaws in character He sees, He is not
disturbed by the emotions that rage through us
He is not perturbed by our failings,
He stands, at the ready, waiting for us to realise.
He stands, not so far away, waiting for us to be honest
He stands, waiting for us to call out to Him in our need
And as we face the honest truth about ourselves, somehow a
release is felt,
the burden of expectation has flown
We expect so much of others, we expect so much of ourselves
Perfection is not the goal we should attain, but love for one
another
Love, love the Lord God, Most High, Creator of all we are, all we
will be, For it is He who has made us.
We wonder why the world is so evil and full of broken lives
For we as people have not loved.
There are those who do love, but in a world that has been handed
over to its own devices
Those who love, struggle against the tide,
Sometimes discouragement can take hold and those who love
wonder why they should continue
We must, we simply must continue
For love is the very threads that hold this world together
And as we come to God in honest truth of ourselves
As we come and lay ourselves before Him

Crying for healing, for comfort, for peace
Crying for the deepest desires of our heart – love
And as we in turn give Him our love
Behold the windows of heaven are being opened
His heart is not one of stone, nor one of steel
But His heart is a heart that beats a rhythm that creation itself
understands
Beneath the flurry of activity, behind the busy schedule of every
man and woman
Behind the tantrum and demand of every child
A beat can be heard
Until we lay aside all the activity
Until we lay aside all the schedules
And listen in the silence for the beat
Listen in the silence for the rhythm
And as we wait, we will hear it coming through
Bdoom...bdoom...bdoom...bdoom...
Our own hearts slow to the rhythm we hear
We breath in time with the rhythm
A sigh escapes
Our shoulders drop
Our bodies feel limp
Weights slide off from every part of our being
And as we wait there, we become aware that we are no longer
alone
For there is One who is close by
He takes us in His arms, a Father and child
We rest our head upon His chest, we hear the heartbeat of God
It thuds like the sea upon the shore, but as gentle as a leaf falling
from a tree
As He holds us, a sigh is heard.
My daughter, my son
Welcome home.

2006

69

Longing

John Caldwell

Longing...

Longing for the day when,
The deaf shall hear and,
The blind shall see and,
The lame will leap for joy,
And the captives are set free.

Longing...

For that day,
When the word goes forth in power,
And the Spirit falls like rain,
Upon the thirsty hearts,
Of those who live in the,
barren land.

Longing...

For that day,
When the church rises up in strength,
Armed with prayer,
and the shield of faith,
and the Sword,
of the Spirit raised high

Longing...
To see them go to war,
Shining bright,
In the midst of darkness,
Trampling on snakes and scorpions,
And all the work of the evil one.

Longing...

For the day, when we march into the enemy's camp,
Releasing the prisoners,
By the power of his word,
And the power of his Blood,
And in the power of his Spirit,
The prison doors swing open wide,
And the captives may go free.

Longing...

For that day,
When we will seek His face,
Humble ourselves and pray,
And turn from our wicked way.

Longing...

For the day when we will see,
The healing rain,
Poured out upon the land.

Longing...

01.2004

Build me a place in your heart

Laura Caldwell

Build me a place in your heart

Where I can come and dwell

Follow the plans that I give

That it might be well

For I will give you all you need

This covenant we share

Build me a place in your heart

And I will meet with you there

For this is the time of the harvest

Now is the time to prepare

Open your heart for my dwelling

And I will meet with you there

2006

Revival Fires Are Coming

John Caldwell

Revival fires are coming,

To spread across the land,

The lamps are burning brighter,

The oil and the wine is prepared,

All that's needed are the vessels.

The vessels are being made ready,

To carry the oil, the fire, and the wine.

01.2004

Like a bird
Laura Caldwell

I was like a bird trapped and caged

And my wings were broken

But words of life and freedom

Into my life You've spoken

You saw me in this place

So afraid and all alone

And You sent Your son Jesus

For my sin He did atone

You've opened up the door

And set my wings in place

So I can fly freely

In Your strength and grace

I'll soar just like the eagle

I'll mount on eagle's wings

For peace and love into my life

Is what your presence brings

2006

God's Presence

John Caldwell

Beautiful, refreshing, accepting, quiet and...

Calm is your presence.

I feel safe in your arms.

Living in the shadows,

your love pursues me.

Settling for less,

looking for satisfaction in broken places –

Your love comes to me and,

Whispers words of grace and mercy.

Knowing my waywardness, struggling with guilt and shame –

Your love surprises and lifts me –

When I deserve it least and need it most.

I am safe in you, I am loved in you,

You know me, and yet you love me.

Teach me your gentle, quiet ways, let me be like you.

Teach me to yield to you.

Teach me to run to you.

Teach me to search for you.

Teach me to listen for you.

Teach me to walk with you.

Break these chains that bind,

By the power of your loving gentle whisper that calms the storm,

Splits the rocks and drives out demons.

Speak your words of love and life to me

Only speak the word, and I shall be free.

Speak the word, Lord. Speak the Word.

You are here, all that matters,

Is you are here.

Nothing compares to you.

Yet I look for satisfaction in desert places.

I need you more than life itself.

You are my life.

Saturate me.

Lay hold of me with your unfailing love.

2004

Sacrifice

Laura Caldwell

It is no sacrifice to do that which is set
Your life's path leads a winding road
Over many trials and through many valleys
Hitting peaks and seeing the magnificence
Of the One who sets feet upon the paths
Often a question may be asked of meaning
Of the journeying that can be so brutal
But also so beautiful
A love so pure
An honesty rarely encountered
Sacrifice of nought compared
To the price settled
To cover me, to redeem me
Jesus
Son of God
Son of man
His sacrifice was exactly that
Sacrifice
A home?
A hillside?
A mountain range?
As I love these it is more the reminder they set
There is One who brought us to that home
There is one who moulded that hillside
One who cut that magnificent mountain range
It is He that I seek
It is Him, His heart I seek
The Giver
His gifts are wonderful and overwhelming
But it is Him I want

30.04.2016

Restore the Roar

John Caldwell

The King's lions have lost their roar,

Their warrior cry is heard no more,

Cowering lions bound by fear –

Their King seems far off, their enemy near.

Bound by lies and intimidation –

Gone is the roar that could wake the nation,

Gone is the boldness – and the desire to fight –

Gone is the roar that puts the enemy to flight!

The enemy knows the power of the roar,

It frees the church, opens prison doors.

The forces of darkness' attacks are violent,

Desperately hoping the lions stay silent.

If only the lions would rise up and roar –

Darkness would flee – the church would soar.

The tide would turn, the sun would rise,

Instead of mourning, there'd be victory cries!

The days of timidity must come to an end,

The Spirit of boldness must descend.

The day of darkness must reign no more,

The time has come to Restore the Roar.

Restore the Roar and watch the enemy run,

Restore the Roar – for Christ has won!

Restore the Roar – see the sick healed,

Restore the Roar – His Glory is revealed.

11.10.2018

Overwhelmed

Laura Caldwell

I am overwhelmed by the peace I feel
My life is not frantic, the rest is real
Not knowing what tomorrow holds in store
No longer causes fear, I don't need to know anymore

For I rest in knowing God has a plan
And that whatever happens, He holds my hand
The fears and doubts that once controlled my life
Only caused me anxiety, stress and strife

I now take pleasure from the smallest of things
Resting in the fact that whatever life brings
God will work it all out, for my best
And so my heart can be at rest

So today I acknowledge and thank God above
For showing me mercy and His unfailing love
For without His part in my life being played
I would have remained broken, sad and afraid

But I've been released from the bonds that held fast
I've broken free, I've escaped at last
My life a testimony to His support and love
I am so grateful to my Father above

2006

Light of His Word

John Caldwell

As a shaft of light,

Dispels darkness. So, your Word,

Drives out my demons.

12.10.2018

The Garden

Laura Caldwell

I come to the garden alone

I come and kneel at Your throne

I lay all aside that would hinder me

I come to the garden alone

Will you come to the garden alone?

Will you come and kneel at His throne?

Will you lay all aside that would hinder thee?

Will you come to the garden alone?

07.2002

Faith

John Caldwell

Faith has the power, to make the wounded whole.

Faith is the way, to rescue our captive soul.

Faith is a duty, but it's also a gift.

Faith, from the slippery pit, your sinking heart will lift.

Faith can move mountains and drown them in the sea,

Forget "seeing is believing", By believing you will see!

Faith says "no" to fear, and "yes" to every promise,

Faith has no time to waste, by being a 'doubting Thomas'.

Faith will lift your hope, higher than a kite,

Faith gives us the victory, for every single fight.

Our faith is not in faith, our faith is in the Lord,

But faith is believing, all that's written in his Word.

If his Word reveals it, it's good enough for me,

By trusting in his promise, from doubt I am set free.

Common sense and logic says. "this is absurd!"

But faith rises higher, by trusting in His Word.

With an air of sophistication, 'Logic' and 'Rationality',

Condemn faith as foolishness – complete insanity.

But 'Rationality', and 'Logic' – as nice as they appear,

They can't save, deliver, heal – or drive away my fear.

Faith renews hope, like flowers blossoming in the Spring,

Faith drives away despair, it will cause your spirit to sing!

Faith comes by hearing, and hearing of God's Word,

Faith will make you soar, like a care-free, happy bird!

12.10.2018

Faith, hope and love

Laura Caldwell

Gotta have a little hope
Gotta have a little love
Gotta have a little faith
Gotta have a little trust

When the storm clouds gather, you can't see the way ahead
You want to turn and run but, you have to stand and fight instead
Believe, only believe, believe, only believe

Your Father knows what's best for you, He knows the path ahead
He can bring life to that which was dead
Believe, only believe, believe, only believe

His plans for you will give you hope
His plans for you are good
His plans for you will give you a future
Won't you believe, won't you believe

Faith, hope and love, won't you have a little
Faith, hope and love, oh have a little
Faith, hope and love
Have a little faith, have a little hope, have a little love

2006 (Song from album: The Best is Yet to Be).

I will not die

Laura Caldwell

I will not die but I will live

to tell what He has done

You did your best to take me out,

but God, He raised me up

You thought you'd won but you were wrong,

for God, He is my song

My God, He is my strength, my rock,

the One who holds my hand

When enemies come to take my life,

right by my side He stands

The Lord, He is my victory,

in Him I can be found

For He has triumphed gloriously,

let's make a joyful sound

2006 (Song from album: The Best is Yet to Be).

From the height of the heavens to the depths of the sea
Laura Caldwell

From the height of the heavens to the depths of the sea

Such is His love that surrounds you and me

As far as the east is from the west

So He's removed my sin from me

No matter where I go in life

No matter what I do

Nothing can ever separate me

Separate me from You

For I am convinced that neither death nor life

No angel or demon or fear

Can ever separate me

From You

27.07.2006

Forever I'll sing of Your love

Laura Caldwell

O Lord You found me, You lifted and ground me,

You loved me and strengthened me

Wrapped Your arms round me

O Lord, forever I'll sing of Your love

And I will sing of the greatest love

That's the love of my God and King

You're the light in the dark

You're the heat in the cold

You're the hope for the lost

Whether young or old

O Lord, forever I'll sing of Your love

You're the strength in the weak

You're the life in the death

You're the bright morning star

You're the giver of breath

O Lord, forever I'll sing of Your love

21.09.2002

The Bible is not a tame book

John Caldwell

No matter who we are,

the Word of the Lord comes as a sword.

Like C.S. Lewis says, "Aslan is not a tame lion",

So the Bible is not a tame book.

We cannot wrestle with it and avoid being pricked by its thorns.

If we try to tame it, sanitise it, or polish it,

we will rob it of its power.

If we think we have reconciled all paradoxes,

solved all exegetical problems,

and harmonised all texts,

we have instead twisted scripture

to suit our own ideas and thinking.

We have robbed it of its power.

We cannot ever claim to have mastered it,

it masters us.

The Bible is not a tame book.

26.09.2006

The Deceiver

Laura Caldwell

"Your life is over"
"Your time is past"
"You'll never be anything"
"Come on, have a blast"
"You've a right to be happy"
"To hell with the rest"
"It's your life"
"You're a long time dead"
"Do what you want"
"Who cares if they condemn?"
"Don't listen to your conscience"
"Do your own thing"
"Look after number one-
"Happiness it will bring"
"You want to enjoy life"
"Gaun – have another drink!"
"It's everyone else that's wrong"
At least that's what you'll think.

STOP listening to deceit!
Stop listening to lies!
For it'll be your downfall,
It'll be your demise.
It's never too late;
You've never gone too far
That a way can't be found
From where you are
For the God who made you
Is calling your name
Start taking responsibility

And stop looking to blame
Your parents, your past,
The things that surround,
But lift up your eyes
And get back on the ground
Start taking steps
Toward the Father
And into His arms
You He will gather

For you are His child
His daughter, His son
The battle has
Already been won
It's the battle of your mind
That carries on
Stop listening to the deceiver
And soon he'll be gone!

2006

Humanity

John Caldwell

Humanity has laughed and cried,

Humanity has smiled and sighed,

Individuals have lived and died.

Sinners spoke truth, saints have lied.

Like Dr Jekyll and Mr Hyde,

We have a good –and dark side.

The warts on our character, we try to mask,

Suppress the demons, paint a smile, in hypocrisy bask.

Cover the truth, people must never see –

The person I try to hide – the real me.

Duality: our unending cursed conflict,

Selfishness springs up, no matter how strict,

I am with myself and try to be good –

Inside my heart, there rages a feud.

Is there no hope?

No way to be free?

Good news comes as revelation –

We need to become a new creation.

The nature of Christ, planted within,

This is the only way to overcome sin.

Like a seed, planted deep, in the soil of our hearts,

Goodness springs up, and darkness departs.

Humanity: a twisted world of harsh hostility and philanthropy,

God: Gives his Son's life, to heal this insanity,

His purpose, His plan? A brand-new humanity –

Where God and people, now dwell in harmony.

13.10.2018

On the outside of my life looking in

Laura Caldwell

There I was on the outside of my life

looking in at a person I just didn't know

Many questions filled my mind, filled my soul,

who am I, what am I, I just didn't know

Who am I? what kind of person do you see

Would you still love if the truth were known of me

God, He broke into my life

and He turned my world around

He's taken all my fear and doubt,

now peace and joy is what I've found

He will do for you, what He has done for me

All you have to do is come and He will set you free

06.2006 (song)

Take a walk on the wild side
Laura Caldwell

Through the fields and forest

I've appreciated the beauty surrounding me

and it's not the outstanding, majestic distant hills,

nor the roll upon roll of lush green pastures,

or the exquisite archways of trees forming over pathways,

but the lone wild flowers that stand alone

that add to the field or forest way

yet they don't stand alone,

for not so far away is another, and another

they are surrounded

by gatherings of various wild flowers also growing

and these are amongst the ever changing grasses,

last week the fields were naturally yellow,

this week the longer grasses with their shades of pink to purple

make the fields appear almost purple,

the grasses so long, I at my 5'10" near disappear

and this is but a very small corner.

I am in awe of God

and His magnificent creation

which groans for His return.

19.06.2017

Humble Sublimity

John Caldwell

Humble Sublimity,
Uniting Paradox,
Limited Infinity,
On earth, walks.

Heaven torn,
Son sent,
King Born,
Highest Descent.

The One who's Eternal,
Entering time,
Embracing the temporal,
Humbly Sublime.

Brightest Light of sun,
Destined for Eclipse,
Dying, Ever-living One,
Darkest death, he grips.

Death consumed,
The Fallen free,
Life resumed,
New Light to see.

Humble Sublimity,
Uniting paradox,
Rescued humanity,
With Divinity walks.

03.12.2015

When my enemy would come against me

Laura Caldwell

When my enemy would come against me

You are there, You are there

When my enemy would come against me

You are there

When I stumble and fall

On Your name I will call

I will call out to You in trouble

I will not be dismayed

For Your hand it is laid

Within mine

10.1992

Bitterness

John Caldwell

Bitterness of soul,

A tragic self-destruction,

Disguised as justice.

13.10.2018

Father I ask

Laura Caldwell

Father I ask for wisdom to know, discernment to see

Strength to continue and passion for Thee

That I may not be lax in my approach to this fight

But that You would reveal all in Your light

The gaps in my armour, the chinks in my sword

Grant me authority and the power of Your word

That as I face my foe in this fight to the death

Help to stand fast until my very last breath

Grant me the steadfastness of Shammah who fought for his patch

The strength of Samson, but not his weakness, fear I catch.

The humility and honour of Jabez, as he cried

"oh that You would bless me" no more pain to hide

I ask for courage, like that of Esther the queen

That even facing death, Your name I'd not demean

But most of all of these above, the precious gift I desire

Is to walk with You in the garden and to move up higher

Grant me intimacy with You, so close we'll breathe in time

My heart beat like Your heart for I'm Yours and You're mine

26/12/2006

Lay down your life

Laura Caldwell

Lay down your life before the Lord and He will raise you up

Just put your hand within His hand and never give up

Just walk along with Him each day and stay close by His side

And underneath His loving arms you can safely hide

1993

Praise and Glory

John Caldwell

Praise is the rising smoke of the fire of
His Love in the heart of His Saints, who are
consumed by His Glory which overwhelms
their vision like the blazing fire which sets
the sea's horizon into a love-scene where
the sun bows down and kisses the ocean
lighting up sea and sky, with ecstatic,
climatic, dancing shifting shades of light.

15.10.2018

Secret place (song of Solomon 2:14)

Laura Caldwell

To the secret place I come

Lord to seek Your face I come

Lord to hear Your voice that is so sweet

For in the secret place I find

Lord Your love and grace, I find

Lord a place of quiet rest

O how I love the secret place

How I long to see Your face

How I love to hear Your voice

In the secret place

29 August 2002

All I want to do

Laura Caldwell

All I want to do
Is to share my life with you, with you

Satan sought to take my life
And all I had was gone
Felt so lonely deep inside
But You prayed for me, prayed for me

Through the valleys low I walked
Burdens on my back
You came and took them from me
And You carried me, carried me

You took me from the desert place
To the mountain high
No matter where I go in life
Your love reaches me, reaches me

Now You are my Father
My truly faithful friend
By my side forever
'til this journey's end, journey's end

29 July 2000

Forgiveness

John Caldwell

Overlooking hurt.

Offering your open hands,

For your foes to pierce.

13.10.2018

When your 'get-up-go' has gone

Laura Caldwell

Ever had a day when your 'get-up-go' has gone?

You want to let go, there's no reason to hold on.

Just you hold fast, this times not gonna last

But out of this will come a strength that will keep you holding on

When your hope has been deflated

and your breath just sucked right out

Just you hold on, it won't be very long,

and push aside the doubt

Your strength will be renewed and soon you will soar

Rising high on the wings of the dawn,

soaring on the wind of this new day

You'll look in awe and wonder, and find no words to say

For you will be speechless in the blessings that God has in store

Overwhelmed by His goodness – and look – there's more!

20.12.2006

Keep on going

Laura Caldwell

Though the way is rough and the climb is high

Hold on to Him and just keep going

He never said it would be easy

He never said it would be smooth

But this one thing He guarantees

His love for you cannot be moved

And when you're down there in the valley

Crying "no, I can't go on!"

Just remember this one thing

He loves you low and high and long

And soon you'll be up on the mountain

Soaring high and feelin' fine

Just don't forget what He says

"I am yours and you are Mine"

2.09.2000

The Cross

John Caldwell

He

was

nailed to a tree. Nails driven through his hands. Fastening
him to a cursed cross. Hung on wood. Hands and feet

secured.

Lifted

up

for all

to see

their

shame.

Son

Of

God

Crucified.

15.10.2018.

Come aside

Laura Caldwell

Come aside and be with Me
Come to Me alone
Come and spend some time with Me
Come and be at one

For I know the plans I have for you
The things I have for you to do
But how will you know? How will you know,
If you don't come?

I see you rush on through each day
Never having time to pray
The world is closing in, the world is closing in
Still you don't come

Now you sit alone and cry
And I hear you asking 'why?'
If only you had come, if only you had come
And been with Me

I will be here standing by
To wipe away the tears you cry
You'll never be alone, you'll never be alone
If you will come

17.02.2001

Up from the wilderness

Laura Caldwell

The Lord led me to a desert place,

a wilderness that was unknown

And I did not understand His reason,

What purpose could there be

In a place so forlorn

I wept,

broken by life,

feeling so alone

Desperate were my cries

In that place of solitude,

I learned of my Saviour

And saw who I was in His eyes

In that place of emptiness

He spoke words so tenderly,

He reset my foundations

Took my broken heart so carefully

In the place of brokenness,

He has healed and made strong

My Saviour, my King

He promised that my valley of trouble would become a gateway of hope

And so it is!

In that desert place I discovered life

People will stand as I come up from the wilderness

A bride of the Most High

I pledged my love anew to my King

He is my Husband, lover of my soul

And a covenant has been made

He will cause me to live unafraid

In peace and in safety

I will be His forever

I will know Him as Lord, with His eyes forever on me

His unfailing love ever toward me

His faithfulness to me

One

He lives to change my world

2006

The Broken Body of Christ

John Caldwell

What on earth, have God's people done?

They've broken the body, that was meant to be one.

Instead of one church, expressing his grace,

They're shattered in a thousand pieces – what a disgrace.

The church is called to be a loving community,

But instead follows a path of endless disunity,

It divides over doctrine, it divides over style,

It's quick to be intolerant, instead of going the extra mile.

One calls itself a kirk, the other calls itself a chapel,

The cause of this feud, is Adam's stolen 'apple'.

The Fall of man, is the root of this division,

When we're defined by difference, we've lost sight of our mission.

One Spirit. One Baptism. One loaf of Bread.

A church divided, is a sign: The Body is dead.

Despite the shame, we continue with the show,

Oblivious to the truth, a divided body can't grow.

But what can be done about this cursed condition?

First we must repent of all godless division.

Then we must fix our gaze on the heavenly vision,

On God, Christ, his cross – the Spirit and Mission.

Then the church will be healed,

The former tribes will unite,

The Glory of God – revealed,

His army, again, will stand and fight,

The demons shall be put to flight,

Sons of darkness will become, sons of light,

Then Jesus shall return – what a glorious sight!

10.2018

In the toilet with Tozer

Laura Caldwell

Divine revelation comes in the strangest places!*

Suddenly I see

As if a light switched on in the darkness

God IS God!

Supreme Lord!

He is not man that He should lie!

He is truth.

His word is true and shall come to be.

We need to know His word

For when the enemy comes, as he did with Eve,

we need to be ready.

If we doubt God's character we are but calling Him a liar.

To doubt God's integrity – what slander.

Human sin began with loss of faith in God

"God deserves and invites unreserved confidence"

"any proper relation to Him must be confidence, that is, by faith"

I see my faulty building is being restored.

Not all discarded but the old charred stones, the truths shall be
used again

Repentance is our apology

How can we distrust God?

Throw yourself upon Christ by faith

Having complete confidence

It is His righteousness.

God's grace by which we can come

He can be trusted.

In Christ alone!

My hope, His love

I am loved by God, dead in my sin He found me

Where sin, death and untruths had bound me

And all through my life, with its trouble and strife

I'll praise God that His love did surround me

19/10/2010

*I wrote this in the wee small hours of the morning, having been up breast-feeding our youngest, I staggered into our toilet and came upon a devotional by A.W. Tozer. I sat there and was able to read with clarity; the words were like water upon a dry and barren land, and the truth that lay therein unravelled a lie that I had been believing. It was a divine moment that pierced the spiritual darkness in which I had been for quite some time. My sense of humour is such that I entitled it - 'In the toilet with Tozer'.

Sacrifice & empty words

Laura Caldwell

Sacrifice and empty words are not what You have asked
But obedience to Your word, this is our only task

Like King David once of old, failed throughout his life
But his heart was set on You, and You blessed his life

Jeremiah was so young, he felt he couldn't speak
But You gave him words to say, strength where he was weak

Peter, he was just the same, always in a state
But he tried over again, and You made him great

In my life be glorified, in my life be glorified today

2.03.2002 (song)

Have you been to the River of God?

John Caldwell

Have you been to the River of God?

Is this the river that flows

from a soul who has had a true revelation of Christ,

who has been convicted of sin and judgement and righteousness

and who has realised the depth of mercy in the cross of Christ?

Is this the river of forgiveness

that comes through the blood of Christ

and penetrates to the deepest part of your being

causing you to be filled with praise, worship and awe

at the presence of the living God?

Is this the river that washes away all fear of man,

death, insecurities, hardness of heart,

and leaves only a healthy fear of God?

Is this the river that washes the redeemed of the Lord

who have turned from their sin and trusted the saviour

and now stand perfect before a Holy God

thanks to the death and resurrection of Jesus Christ?

If so, I've been to the river.

27.03.2002

Awaken

Laura Caldwell

Awaken my soul, a new song has come

It's time to get ready, this song must be sung

Having sat in the darkness with no hope in sight

Behold Christ has come, with His word and His light

Arise weary soul, take the hand of the Master

It's time to get up, it's not a disaster

The struggle has brought, the wings as intended

Break out, break out, the long night has ended

Sing o my soul, sing a new song

The darkness is lifting, though it's been so long

Lay hold of God's word, it's your sword for the fight

Stand firm on God's promises, His word keeps you right

Sing o soul, sing a new song

The long night is over, behold a new dawn

Sing, sing, prepare the new song

For the long night is over, behold a new dawn

(In the toilet with Tozer)

19/10/2010

Your Cross Alone

John Caldwell

May I dare not trust in anything,

but to your cross, alone I cling,

And once again my heart will sing,

Your righteousness, my everything

01.15.2007

In the dark of night

Laura Caldwell

In the dark of the night

When no man knows your mind

And no eye see the tears that you cry

In the depths of despair

Do not fear, I'll be there

I will carry you

In my arms of love

Nestle in, hear my heart,

Feel it beating so hard

My child, this heart is for you

If only you could know the love that's in my heart for you

Never would you doubt my word, or my promises were true

Listen hear, my child

Come near, my child

Stay with me and learn to know

My love for you is higher than the heavens

Deeper than the sea

Vaster than the east and west

Beyond this galaxy

For you are mine, my child, my love

09.2006 (song)

Lift your vision higher

John Caldwell

Is your God the God of the living and not the dead? If not
lift your vision higher.
Is Jesus Christ the same yesterday and today and forever? If not
Lift your vision higher.
Have you received Christ yet you're walking in darkness? If so
Lift your vision higher.
Do you recognise that if you're born again, greater is He that lives
in you and that you are seated in heavenly places far above all
rulers,
principalities and powers of darkness? If not
Lift your vision higher.
Do you know that if Christ lives in you he will do "greater works "
through you if you fully surrender and walk in faith not fear? If not
Lift your vision higher.
Do you know that if you're a real Christian you may be the only
Bible people ever read? If not
Lift your vision higher.
Do you know that God is calling you to a great and mighty work in
these last days? if not
Lift your vision higher.

Do you know that God still does miracles if we ask and trust in

Jesus' name? If not

Lift your vision higher.

Do you know that you are precious and loved by God the father,

Son and Holy Spirit, the three in one God? If not

Lift your vision higher.

Do you know that Satan has no authority in your life if you're a

child of GOD? If not, fix your eyes on Christ and

Lift your vision higher!

Do you know that these are the last days and the ark is ready and

the trumpet is ready to be sounded? Have you heard the trumpet

call to repentance and faith in the Son of God? Respond today and

Lift your vision higher!

2002

Do we serve a God who is not able?

Laura Caldwell

Do we serve a God who is not able?

Or a God who does not hear?

Do His eyes not observe?

Do we serve a God of fear?

NO.

We serve a God who calms the storm to a whisper and stills the turbulent seas

What a blessing was that stillness, that He brought to me.

He turns the deserts into pools of water, the dry land into flowing springs

He brings the hungry to settle there, to build, to sow, a harvest He brings

Blessed are those who walk with the Lord, in Him their life is complete

He shall take away their sorrow, and make their life sweet

Your life shall no more be a desert, no more hungry but full

From bare shall be blessing, no longer barren but fruitful.

22.12.2006

Who is Like you?

John Caldwell

Who is like you?

Majestic in Holiness,

Awesome in Glory,

Working wonders.

2007

Last night as you wept

Laura Caldwell

Last night as you wept, He stood close by
As you fell asleep with the exhaustion of emotion
He watched
Wanting to take you in His arms
To hold you
This is a time of preparation
Of rebuilding
Of restoring
But also of breaking
So things can be reset
Refocused
Made right
Don't think that God is not there
Don't think that He has left you alone
He is all around you
He watches over you as you sleep
And says, "rest"
As you come to Him, as you pursue Him
He will be found by you
He will not let you stumble and fall
He will protect you
He will watch over you Himself
He will stand by your side as your protective shade
He will keep you from all evil and preserve your life
He will watch over you
Always
And forever

2005

The Lord is my shepherd

Laura Caldwell

The Lord is my shepherd, I have all I need

By the green meadow and stream He does lead

My strength is renewed as I wait on Him

Over mountain and through valley I'll follow Him

My desire is that I honour Him

Give Him the glory due to His name

My heart's desire is that I might know Him

He is my Lord, He's always the same

When darkness appears and troubles surround

In His unfailing love, I can be found

For He'll never go, never leave my side

He is my refuge, my help, my Guide

May 2006

ABOUT THE AUTHORS

John and Laura Caldwell live in Perthshire, loving the semi-rural landscapes that surround, with their two sons, Ethan and Caleb, and their crazy, loving lab, Calvin. Laura is a home-maker, and sole trader of a craft and jewellery business, *Remnant Designs*. John is a school teacher, a preacher, and a Bible-teacher, who ministers God's word across various local churches throughout Scotland. They married in 2007 and believe their marriage was made in heaven and is being refined on earth.

22258344R00076

Printed in Great Britain
by Amazon